A QUARL

A QUARE GEG

John Pepper

Illustrations by Rowel Friers

BLACKSTAFF PRESS

First published in 1979
by The Blackstaff Press
3 Galway Park, Dundonald, Belfast BT16 0AN
This reprint edition 1984

© John Pepper 1979, 1984
All rights reserved
Printed in Northern Ireland by
Belfast Litho Printers Limited

ISBN 0 85640 193 5

Contents

List of Illustrations

A Word from the Author

Join me in yet another expedition into the inviting, if sometimes bizarre byways of Ulster speech. Every journey along these eternally beguiling corridors of word-power produces new surprises for me.

It proves beyond question that Northern Ireland is a Disneyland of terminological delight. An approach to language which leads to a friend being greeted in the street with 'Don't tell me it's you!' is one small token of its enchantment.

Once again my thanks go to the considerable number of people good enough to regard me as a repository for their favourite examples of lively and genial use of words. My debt to them for allowing me to borrow their ears is beyond price.

They are everywhere, eavesdropping, missing nothing, and they show that there are rich pickings. The air in Ulster is not filled alone with the sound of gunfire and abuse, anger and malice.

A 'thick Belfast accent' is often spoken of with disparagement. The Belfast undertones in the speech of such figures well-known in their respective fields, as James Galway, John Watson, Frank Carson and George Best are recognisable to all Ulstermen, yet none of them is on record as saying they are ashamed of their heritage.

It may be argued that some of the illustrations I quote with such pleasure may be heard in other areas, in other accents, and are not exclusive to any one community. It could easily be said that many had their beginnings in Northern Ireland and spread from there.

To my mind it is not unreasonable to lay claim to them if they fall naturally into the Ulster style of speech.

John Pepper

'A lake is a hole in a kettle.'

There is nothing exceptional about the Belfastwoman of whom it was said 'She's going through one of her phrases.' Unforeseen phrases come naturally to women's lips in Ulster. They come in all shapes and sizes, at the drop of a hat.

It is a community where speech is not just a means of communication. It may also be used to cause confusion and bewilderment, to confound those who aren't in the know.

Besides it can put such people in their place.

There may be other regions where you are apt to be continually stumped if you don't speak the language. In Ulster you may resign yourself to going around in a perpetual daze if you lack a thorough knowledge of the idiosyncrasies of the Province's native speech.

The truth is that it is a word wonderland, a place where the misnomer is congenital, and the solecism is supreme.

It comes from a way with language brimming over with the unpredictable — as well as the enchanting — a way that is an eye-opener to anyone encountering it for the first time.

It should be pointed out, perhaps, that the unexpected observation is not entirely confined to the ladies. It only appears so because usually they seem to have much more to say.

The little girl who was asked 'What is a lake?' and replied, 'A hole in a kettle,' and the woman who said, 'I was near myself,' were making their own distinctive contribution to the confusion.

Each was demonstrating how a mixture of the vernacular and the observation of certain conventions add up to an extravaganza of speech quite indigenous to the area.

In fact one was referring to a leak; the other was putting into her own words a narrow escape from disaster.

The visitor who asked his way to a particular street in Belfast and was told,

'It's down there on the left, beside the wriggley tin,' was encountering a fairly common reluctance to use the recognised term. What was being referred to was a corrugated iron fence. 'Wriggley tin' is much less stilted.

To use the phraseology of the man chatting to a friend at a Belfast bus stop, 'Ye hafta reckanise that we're funny.'

An Ulsterman will tell you, 'I'm hoarse listenin' to the wife,' convinced he is making a revelation that will hold your attention — as well as earn your sympathy.

His wife will suggest to a visitor, 'Put yourself on a piece of toast,' confident that the guest will have the wit to appreciate that it is not an invitation to be taken literally, and that the intention is entirely hospitable.

Excusing her child's absence from school a mother will send a note saying, 'The wee sowl's stummick's heavin'.' The teacher will know at once that the lad has indigestion.

There is a directness of its own about the statement of the lady from the Falls Road who said of a neighbour's noisy youngster, 'I saw him waltzing down the street whistlin' at the top of his voice.'

She comes from the same vernacular line of country which produces such announcements as, 'I'll have a wee lie down to rest my eyes,' and the request made by a caller at an optician's, 'I want a pair of sunglasses for my head's jumpin'.

It is a safe guess that it was the same speaker who complained to a friend, 'Know this? I was up half the night with Jack's toothache.'

Should you find yourself in a crowded Belfast shop and a woman comes up to you, saying, 'Would you let me by you?', it doesn't mean that she wants to spend money on a present for you. She just wants to get past and be on her way.

Basically, the aim of these pages is simply to guide the stranger's faltering footsteps once more through the language labyrinth to be encountered in Ulster, to help to show that the Queen's English is there constantly used quite differently, certainly no less imaginatively, to what is considered acceptable in other parts of the English-speaking world.

It seeks to help towards understanding, for example, that when someone says to you, 'You're a quare geg' it can mean:—

(a) 'You're a right chancer.'
(b) 'Boys, but you take me for a right idiot.'
(c) 'You're a bit of an innocent, aren't you?'
(d) 'Why don't you catch yourself on.'
(e) 'Are you right in the head?'
(f) 'Why don't you take a running jump?'

'*Put yourself on a piece of toast.*'

The charge may be made that there is nothing particularly noteworthy about what might be termed vulgar speech. It can be argued that it glamourises the ungraceful to suggest that it is picturesque to say of someone who has been unwell, 'He wuz vamitin'.'

But while *what* is said is more important than *how* it is said, there are exceptions; even if the average reaction to the statement, 'The wee lad threw up the stairs,' is not 'I wish I'd said that.'

My view, nevertheless, is that while it may appear that Ulster people live and have their being in a linguistic no man's land, they cannot be dismissed as language louts.

They have as much right — often a great deal more — to take pride in their way of speech as the Texan, the Geordie, the Australian, the Yorkshireman, or even the Bristolian.

'I want to see the borr.'

Anyone seeking either to become a fluent speaker of Norn Iron or to understand it thoroughly must observe certain rules. These sometimes follow a set pattern, often they do not. They are wide-ranging and not always predictable.

Take the words in which the letters *th* come together. The convention in Ulster when this happens is to treat them as expendable. Yet while it converts 'mother' into 'morr' it will also be found that 'borrow' is transformed into 'borr'.

Nevertheless the rule helps to explain the use of 'Nivver borr', in other words avoid taking the action you had intended.

It accounts for the difficulty in which the headmaster of a Co Armagh school found himself when a young woman was shown into his study, announcing urgently, 'I want to see the borr.'

The baffled head, an Englishman only a few weeks in the post, eventually led the visitor off into the school's interior and showed her the boiler. He then discovered he was being given his first lesson in Norn Iron. The caller was in search of 'the brother'.

It mastery of the Ulster vernacular is to be assured it is important to recognise the specific principles involving the use of the letter *a*. It is constantly made to act as a substitute for *o*.

This is the reason for such inquiries as, 'Cud a barr a poun' aff ye?'. It converts 'See you tomorrow' into 'Seeya the marra', and ensures that anyone called 'Dorothy' must resign herself to answering to 'Darathy'.

'Fally me' means 'Follow me' and 'Ahafta' is an example of running together the words, 'I will have to.' It saves time.

The intrusive *a* is thrust into a thousand and one expressions. It isn't always easy, however, to spot the occasions when the rule of *a* is strictly observed.

'You're a harrid little man' loses none of its bite if uttered in the Ulster fashion, 'Yer harrid.' 'I'm sorry' acquires an emphasis of its own when it takes the form of, 'Ach a'm awful sarry so a am.'

A visitor to Belfast was convinced she was hearing Hindustani when a woman bus passenger, wearing a fur coat, was being bothered by a small child in the seat behind who was busily sucking a lollipop. As can happen, the lollipop kept jabbing into the fur coat and the wearer swung round to voice her irritation. Doubtless it was 'stimulated fur', widely worn in the province.

'Minnie', the mother addressed the youngster, 'wud ye stap flaffin' yer lally.'

Other results of the *a* precept are to generate such contortions as 'watter' for 'water'. Even 'waltz' is affected in an upside down way for it is reincarnated as 'wallace', pronounced as in 'Alice'.

The statement, 'I saw him claps,' does not mean that someone was seen in the act of applauding. All it does is explain that the speaker watched a man collapse in the street.

Appreciation of the rule of *a* will make clear why a Belfastman will speak of 'Ar MP,' 'Ar street', 'Ar house,' as well as 'We're away for ar dinner,' and 'It's time for ar tea.'

A classic example of this feature of Norn Iron was the experience of a Belfat teacher who asked her class to write a composition about their summer holidays. One offering began, 'We went on ar holidays to the Alafman.' Imagining that her pupil had been to some exotic and little-known part of North Africa, the teacher read on with great interest only to be deflated when the essay expounded the delights of Douglas, Port Erin and the big wheel at Laxey.

Not uncommon is the use of 'Ack' to indicate impatience, or annoyance that the memory of a name or an article eludes the speaker as in, 'Ack, I should know what they call him but I can't think of what it is.'

There is a bluntness about 'I will nat' lacking in the more formal usage, just as 'I gat my stackins japped' introduces its own variant of vehemence.

An interesting tendency is to drop the *a* completely in such phrases as 'a week', 'a fortnight'. This generates 'The day after the marra.'

'I have a slate aff' sounds like a frank admission of lack of mental

'Minnie, wud ye stap flaffin' yer lally.'

stability. In fact the words are often used by Housing Executive tenants grumbling about damage after a storm.

An official to whom one such complaint was made obviously had a sense of humour. 'Don't worry, missus,' he told the complainant, 'I won't tell a soul.'

Another convention is the tendency to forget the *d* where it ends a word.

'Lennus' is Norn Iron for 'lend me' and 'Cud ye menn these shoes?' indicates the need for them to be soled and heeled.

The principle also begets such admonitions as 'Mine where yer goin,' 'Mine outa the road,' and 'Mine yer head.'

It is important for the student to observe the maxim which turns *n* into *m*.

'You've been on the foam for the last half hour,' doesn't mean you have been away at sea, just that you have been an unduly long time on the telephone, running up the bill.

'To' is often used in preference to 'till' as in 'Wait to I tell you'.

'Again' is frequently regenerated as 'agayun', and there are such contortions as 'goodbyway' for the more simple 'goodbye', 'ba-ake' for 'bake' and 'warsey?' for 'Where is he?'

'Wegatanorn' is Ulsterese for 'We got another one.'

The *d* is made utterly superfluous in the case of the word 'old'. Pronounced 'owl' is develops affectionate undertones as in 'This bit of an owl coat', 'The owl lad,' 'It's a funny owl day,' 'These owl boots is great' and 'I like puttin' on this owl hat.'

Useful in adding weight to a statement is the introduction of 'right'. You will be told of 'a right bitch', when it is sought to emphasise dislike. Other forms are 'He's a right miser', 'He's a right dunderhead', and 'You're a right ijit', as well as the generally used 'Right Charlie'.

The tendency to save time by running words together is followed as eagerly in Northern Ireland as in Scotland.

It brought a moment of bewilderment for a new assistant minister accosted on the Shankill Road by a parishioner. 'Yenohimamgoinwi?' he was asked.

He gave her a blank look as the speaker went on, 'Hisdasdead.

It meant simply that the father of the young woman's boy friend had passed away.

The addiction was to blame for a shop assistant's call to a colleague in the upstairs part of a Belfast shop 'Alluuckennagup', in other words, 'I'll look when I go up.'

It gave birth to the Biblical extravaganza, uttered by a small boy during a Sunday school lesson, 'Jassesisriz'.

And the announcement about a trader who managed to stay in business after his shop had been the target of a terrorist bomb, 'His shap riz from thashes.'

It was also behind the frantic cry of a woman passenger who found herself on the wrong bus, 'Lettusaff Sawaythawrangway.'

'Thereyarni' implies that you have only yourself to blame for the dilemma in which you find yourself. Translated it says, 'There you are now.'

It is important that a visitor should have a clear understanding, when asking the way, that the place he seeks may sound at variance with the real thing.

A useful decoder to the difficulties this can produce is to be aware of the fact that:

> Atlantic Avenue becomes Clantic Avenue
> Botanic Avenue becomes Tonic Avenue
> Damascus Street becomes Mascus Street
> Grosvenor Road becomes Governor Road
> Massey Avenue becomes Messey Avenue
> Ormeau Road becomes Ormer Road
> Soxth Street becomes Sick Street
> Tate's Avenue becomes Tayes Avenue
> Tennent Street becomes Tent Street
> Hollywood Arches becomes Tharches
> Newtownards Road becomes Newnarge Road.

How to feel at home.

A persistent problem facing the stranger in any community is the tendency to be regarded with suspicion, an outsider to be treated cautiously.

He is an interloper, an intruder. It is constantly borne on him that he is an import. If he goes shopping he is at a disadvantage. If his speech emphasises that he is not 'one of us' he is fair game if bargaining is involved.

Should he be sensitive, aware of how easily he can put his foot in it and be clearly shown to be the odd man out, the situation can be highly uncomfortable.

The following guidelines are designed to help the visitor to feel at home in Northern Ireland when being entertained, shopping, discussing the weather, or eating out.

Listed here is way the stranger would speak, the form in which an Ulster speaker would put it, and, in italics, imitated pronunciation. It is useful to avoid pauses between syllables when simulating North Iron.

WHEN GOING SHOPPING

Aren't you looking rather much for this article?

The price you're asking is ridiculous. *Away-or thon. Doanbe dicalas.*

This watch I bought isn't keeping proper time.

This owl watch you sowl me keeps stappin'. *This oul bitaffa watch you sowl me has started stappin' so it has.*

I had trouble finding a trolley at the supermarket.

There was such a rush that the tralleys were hard to come by. *I cudden fine a tralley for lovver money.*

Those shoes would be much too small for me.

Them shoes would never fit me. *Them shoes wudden luck on me.*

VISITING

Did you say tea was ready?

Is the tea wet? *Isn't-the-tay-wet-yitt?*

I'm afraid I'm a teetotaller.

I never touch it. *Ach-a-nivver-lippit.*

I think you should be on your way.

It's time you were on your one end. *Stime ye wur on yir wunnend.*

She doesn't look her age.

She stands it well. *She's stannin it ritely.*

He's a silly wee man.

He has a wee want. *That fella's a stupid ijit.*

Please could I get past?

Would you get out of the road? *Wud ye let me by?*

It is quite near.

It's no more than a mile or two.

'*Ach-a-nivver-lippit.*'

	It's onney two or three spits down the road.
Thank you but I have just had a cup of tea.	It's all right. I'm just after a cup. *Sawlrite I'm onny after gettin.*
I hope your husband is in good health.	Is himself all right? *An' how's hisself?*

ILLNESS

If you aren't careful you'll catch pneumonia.	You'll only get your end if you don't watch. *Mine out. You'll onny catch your en'.*
She's feeling poorly.	She's not at herself. *The sowl's nat atterself.*
She's in a critical condition.	Sure she's waitin' on. *The poor thing's waitin' on.*
She took ill through overwork.	She took bad keeping her pan in. *She tuk bad knockin' her pannin.*
She had a lengthy illness.	She was lying a quare while. *She was laid up ferages.*
Could you give me something for an upset stomach?	Could I have a bottle for throwing off? *Givvus a battle for vamitin'.*
My husband has kidney trouble.	My man's in bed with his kidneys. *The oul lad's laid up with his kidleys — an' ye know why? He threw aff a pullover.*
She feared the worst.	She was sure she was sent for. *She thought she was senfir.*
We're waiting for his recovery.	We're waiting for him to come till. *Ach we're hangin' on till he comes till.*

THE WEATHER

It's pouring.

It isn't half coming down. *Snat haff cummin' down.*

It looks like rain.

It's spittin' so it is. *Spittin'.*

That's a really cold morning.

It's a bitter kind of a day. *Spitter. It wud skin a ferry.*

It's a light shower.

It's just a wee skiff. *Ach it's onny a wee bit affa skiff.*

MISCELLANEOUS

We're hoping to move house soon.

We're plannin' a flit. *We're flittin' in a fortnight.*

He doesn't appear terrible well educated.

He's an ignorant glype. *That fella's an iggerant glype.*

Someone has taken my plimsolls.

A thief has tuk my gutties. *My gutties is neuked.*

'Them legs is in your road.'

Knowledge of the code governing everyday speech in Northern Ireland may be a tremendous help to the visitor but in the end it is not enough. There are occasions when rules simply do not apply, when they are quietly dropped.

It is impossible to anticipate the kind of inquiry made by a man armed with a spade who called at a house in Co Down and inquired seriously, 'You don't know anybody round here who doesn't want no diggin' done?' It follows the pattern which gives rise to 'You wouldn't have a match on you, would you?'

In the same unpredictable class is the comment overheard in a Belfast street. Two women were walking along together when one stumbled and fell. As her companion helped her to her feet she said, 'You're always doing that. Them legs is in your road.'

A Londonderry man was asked by a friend, 'Are you aff the beer?'

'I'm still on it when I can get it,' was the answer, 'but aff it when I can't so put that intil the saucepan of your head and tell us what answer you get.'

A commercial traveller was grumbling to a prospective customer about the difficulty he had in finding him in his office.

'There's some days,' came the explanation, 'when I'm out for the better part of a week.'

The woman who was heard to say, 'I'd know Jimmy if his feet were stickin' out of a barrel,' was putting her own emphasis on her familiarity with the man.

And the bar-tender who was having difficulty in removing the cork from a bottle summed up his frustration in his own style by saying, 'Dammed if I'm goin' to let it bate me. I'll get this owl cork out if I have to put it in.'

There was a touch of the unexpected about the reply given by a porter to an inquiry about train times. 'If you don't want to wait for a train there's a bus every other hour on the half-hour. But the train will get you there first.'

An inability to give properly co-ordinated directions is a common Ulster weakness. One motorist who had gone off course was gravely advised, 'Keep on down the road there and watch out on the right till you come to a big cheeser tree on the corner of a big wide avenue. But don't go down there. For God's sake don't do that. The one you want is away past that on the left. Just ast anybody.'

Again, 'Last week at the market he drunk a sow and its whole litter,' should not be taken as implying an exceptional digestion. The words indicate that the man concerned visited a pub and there spent the money obtained from the sale of the sow and its young.

One feature of Ulster speech lacks any special significance and none should be attached to it. When such statements as 'I don't want anything, like' are made it should be understood that the 'like' is really superfluous, something thrown in purely for effect. What the precise effect might be is not quite clear.

'I was playing a game of cards, like.'
'I was coming home in the bus, like.'
'I was going to the match, like.'
'I was lighting my pipe, like.'
'I was at the pictures, like.'
'I was on my bike, like.'

Phrases like these may be regularly heard, all illustrating the persistence of the habit, like.

The use of the word has the same pointlessness as the tendency to ask questions to which the answer is patently obvious.

On reaching a house of a meeting place where you are expected the

'I'd know Jimmy if his feet were stickin' out of a barrel.'

chances are that you will be greeted with the query, 'Have you arrived?'

Call someone on the phone and instead of hearing a responsive 'Hello' you are liable to be assailed with the question, 'Were you ringing?'

A person walking along the street with an arm in a sling is almost certain to be asked, 'Did you hurt yourself?' If the trouble is a sprained ankle and entails the use of a walking stick the inquiry is bound to be made, 'Are you limping?'

Similarly, someone just back from a stay on the Continent, and with a tan to emphasise the fact, will be asked, 'Are you back from your holidays?'

The ramifications are endless. A husband arriving home, soaking, on a pouring night will be faced with the challenge, 'Are you wet?'

A shopkeeper will throw open the doors of his establishment first thing in the morning and he can depend on the first customer to arrive wanting to know, 'Are you open?'

It is on a par with the inquiry put to the woman lying prone on the pavement, 'Did you fall?'

The convention follows the lines of the tendency to use the word 'very' as a kind of portmanteau expression to add special emphasis.

The statement will be heard, 'It happened in this very room.' Someone will say, 'This is the very day.' Other variations are, 'He's the very man,' 'This is the very ticket,' 'That's the very car,' 'This is the very street.'

However, I have yet to hear one of the travellers who use the Strangford boat coming out with, 'This is the very ferry.'

Extravagant use is also given to 'wee' as an all-embracing adjective. It is brought into use on every conceivable occasion, not as a substitute for 'small' but largely through habit.

'A wee busybody' does not imply the size of the person referred to, just as 'a wee ruffian' can be used in respect of a hulking young brute. 'A wee gossip' means a gossip of considerable venom.

A 2,500cc Rover could become 'a right wee car' but 'a wee horse' doesn't mean that a pony is meant.

There is its own element of the bewildering about the comment of a woman at a Belfast market. She was surrounded by four small children and was heard instructing the eldest of them, a boy of seven, 'Alec, will ye go an' luck for yir father and when ye find him tell him he's lost?'

And it is impossible not to listen with a feeling of wonder to the woman who was shown a photograph of a friend's small son and said, 'He's that like you it would scare you.'

'He's a single man. He never married.' is another example of the tendency to emphasise the obvious, an instinct forever thrusting itself into the forefront.

This is not to say that the obvious cannot sometimes be given a touch of sarcasm.

A witness in a court case said, 'I saw him jukin' roun' the corner. I saw him wi' my own eyes.'

'Jukin'? What's jukin'?' was the inquiry from the Bench.

'Surely,' was the impatient response, 'you know what a juke is?'

One convention enables the use of the word 'Bully' to imply praise, acceptance, approval. If a girl hears the greeting 'Bully Rosie' she knows at once that friendliness is being indicated. 'Bully Harry' means that Harry is completely acceptable. 'Bully George' means that George is considered a hail fellow well met.

But the shop assistant who was asked, 'Would you have the morrow of this glove?' rarely needs to have it pointed out that the inquiry has nothing to do with the day of the week.

To be informed by a woman cleaner, 'I should have sprinkled water on these stairs to lay the sture,' is another way of giving you an apology for the dust.

Most outsiders, however, would be able to grasp the sense of the letter sent to a Department of Health and Social Services official by a farmer involved in a pension claim.

He had been asked to call and give a detailed explanation of his circumstances. Later he was notified that a reduction would have to be made in the amount he argued was his due.

The news inspired a long and abusive missive which concluded with the words, 'If I had of knew what youse wanted hell roast the come I would have went.'

'I don't want to have the family down with semolina.'

Going shopping in Northern Ireland is not just a simple matter of setting out to buy something you need — and obtaining it as quickly as possible.

While the supermarket has introduced a new element in the process, certain social customs come into play which are not easily dislodged.

Shopping means an encounter with friends and neighbours. It provides an opportunity to exchange opinions, to gossip, to see and be seen. The Ulster shopper has her eyes skinned and her ears alert. She missed nothing.

Whether a big downtown store, a hypermarket, or the corner shop is involved, a unique opportunity is provided, one to be eagerly grasped.

A thesis on butchering terms published in the Journal of the Centre for English Cultural Tradition and Language at Sheffield University said that twenty-five different names were used in ordering a cut of brisket in England.

The orders given in Northern Ireland at the butcher's would cover a field no less wide. Sometimes the terms leave even the expert at a loss.

This happened in one establishment where the order was for chitlings.

A hasty conference behind the counter culminated in the assistant asking, 'Missus, would it be guts ye want?'

A different misunderstanding arose when a small boy entered a Belfast grocery store and asked, 'Cud ye givvus somethin' for m'da's piece?'

It was a new assistant and he stared at the boy in surprise, convinced the lad was in search of something for his father's mistress.

Shopping is an exercise full of surprises in Ulster. An experienced shop assistant won't turn a hair when faced with a request for 'A turned down boy's pair of socks.'

An order for Saxa salt can bring its own undertones. If someone asks for 'Sexy salt' it is known instantly what is sought. But if the inquiry runs, 'Do you sell Saxa salt?' the obvious answer is, 'No, missus, we only sell it in packets.'

The clever answer, however, doesn't always work.

'Do you keep red flannel?' a woman asked.

'No, missus,' she was told. 'We sell it.'

A request for 'a tie that wud fit me' must be met with a straight face, just as smooth handling is called for when a woman buying a cap for her husband is asked what size he takes.

'Och now sure it's you is asking me,' could be the answer, 'an' him a man that always bought his own, except the day, when he's workin' at the hay like a Trojan. To be sure, son, I haven't a penny clue but he wears a sixteen collar if that wud be any help to ye.'

It was different when two men were involved in the purchase of non-metric headgear.

One was asked what size he took and replied, 'Six seven eight.'

When the same query was put to his companion the answer came, 'Givvus a seven eight nine for I have a bigger head nor him.'

Situations like this give rise to the description of the shopkeeper of whom it was said, 'He's that kine of a fella if ye wanted a cap he'd sell ye a hard hat.'

Encounters when shopping produce unexpected admissions, as in the case of one shopper who was heard asking an acquaintance, 'Tell me this and tell me no more. Is the tinned salmon all right? I hafta be sure for I don't want to have the family down with semolina.'

The odd request is always liable to be made. It could be for 'anniversity cards', 'a tin of Harrogate beans', even 'a coffee copulator'.

In one case an order for a pair of Spencer Tracey pyjamas was correctly worked out as a quest for a pair made by Marks and Spencer.

A woman who sought a packet of firelighters was asked, 'Do you want them at 10p or 25p?'

'The 10p will do rightly,' she said. 'Sure they're only for lightin' the fire.'

Even shopping lists can feature the unexpected. One in an Ulster country town ran

'1 tin brown blacknin'
'1 pot marmalade jam.
'1 lb margarine butter.
'Bottle of syphon because grannie's not herself.'

Shopkeepers, of course, have their own problems. As one of them put it, 'There's days when I sell nathin' and other days when I wud sell twice as much.'

Probably he was the kind of trader who knew what was expected of him when a customer wrote in relation to a delayed order, 'If you have already sent it you'll know what to do as it didn't get here and if you haven't there's no hurry.'

Few Ulster shopkeepers would have difficulty in dealing with the customer who asked the price of a particular article and was asked, 'Are they in the window?'

'Aye,' she answered. 'Thur thur thur.' Otherwise 'There they are there'.

When it becomes a family affair shopping brings its own complications.

A couple were buying a suit for their small son. Obediently the youngster appeared before them wearing one which the mother thought was just the ticket.

'I don't know,' said the father doubtfully. 'See him? Sure the wee lad's drownin' in that suit so he is.'

A teenager discussing the dresses she was shown explained, 'I don't like the cheap ones. They do nathin' for me.'

Customs may change but a lot of Ulster women still buy their husband's clothes. Traditionally shopping is left to the womenfolk in many cases.

A woman buying a shirt, a pair of socks and winter underwear for her husband explained to the assistant, 'He can be that fussy. Ye'd hardly believe how fussy that man is. But I'll say this for him. He often pays me a compliment so he does. When the spirit moves him. Many's a time he tells me how far-seeing I was to have married him.'

Not quite in the same class was the lady who arrived to pay the last instalment on a pram.

'It's paid for now,' she said triumphantly. 'At long last.'

'And how's the baby keeping?' inquired the shopkeeper.

'The best. I'll be bringin' her roun' next week to see you. She's gettin' married next month.'

A woman complained to a neighbour, 'I bought wee Jimmy a new per av trousers last week there and d'ye know he had the behine outa both knees almost before he put them on.'

It is possible she had the same simplistic approach to language as the lady up from the country on a Belfast shopping expedition. She asked a passer-by, 'Cud ye tell me where Bootses is?' and gave no sign whatever that she expected a different answer when told, 'You'll see a shop further along that sells shoeses. It's just a coupla doors away.'

The more rural the area the greater the interest asking the way can arouse. It can even start a dialogue, as in:

'Could you tell me where the Post Office is please?'

'The Post Office? You want to go to the Post Office?'

'That's right. The Post Office.'

'An' what wud ye be wantin' till find the Post Office for? Wud it be stamps, mebbe, or a Postal Order?'

'Neither, in fact. Where exactly is it?'

'Oh I can tell you where it is all right. I was in last week gettin' my television licence.'

'I already have a TV licence.'

'Is that so? They're not chape so they aren't. I always watch the warr forecasts just to see how wrong they are.'

'Is that so?'

'Luck, mister. I'll walk ye down till the Post Office. It's not far. An' what's your favourite programme?'

'Are you readin' that paper you're sittin' on?'

When an Ulsterman moves away from his native surroundings his mannerisms automatically go with him, even if it is clear that they stick out like a sore thumb. They tend to persist, no matter how long the years of exile, a treasured link with his past, not to be cast lightly aside.

He will stick to his instinctive habit of pouring a bottle of stout from left to right, rather than right to left; retain his tendency to jab a listener in the shoulder to emphasize a point; and hold fast to his shuffling style of walking inherited from marching to the rhythm of 'The Sash'.

Ulster people are not exceptional in clinging to their speech usages. Minorities everywhere hold fast to their own special way of putting things. It is part of their identity. It stresses that they are not faceless.

A Belfast holidaymaker in an Italian resort noticed with alarm a small boy chewing a plastic soldier.

'If ye swally that ye'll know all about it,' she warned.

He gave her an enormous smile and offered her a chew.

A slight misunderstanding was caused on a Midlands car factory shop floor when a Co Antrim worker gave as his excuse for being late, 'My wife's tuk to her bed.'

A request few shopkeepers outside Ulster would really appreciate took the form of, 'I'll have a whole lock of that.'

This would also apply to the comment of an Ulsterwoman buying a blanket in a London West End store, 'They're a quare hap on a winter's night.'

English ears would have similar difficulty in appreciating the significance of such comments as,

'The wife give me the rounds of the kitchen last night.'

'Them shoes she bought weren't the right size. Sure she took three or four steps before they even started to move.'

The Ulsterman who insisted 'I've enjoyed bad health all my days' is not always conscious when abroad that the words usually produce a bewildered look. He sees no reason why they should.

Eyebrows were raised on a London bus after a Belfast couple got on board. They had to take separate seats, the one nearest the door buying two tickets. When the conductor approached her companion, sitting further along the vehicle, there was a sudden call to her, 'Sall rite, Aggy. Yours is gat.'

Anyone described as 'a funny bein'' is not necessarily a comedian, and the statement 'She's gone to scrapins' certainly does not indicate that the lady concerned has left on a Continental holiday.

There are similar elements of confusion in the words of a woman discussing her husband's corns. 'Sure he has no hauns for his feet at all,' she complained. The poor chap clearly had paring problems.

Summing up the trials of living in one of Belfast's more troubled areas a woman confided to a relative with whom she was spending a few days in London, 'Me? I wouldn't answer the door at night for all the tea in China and I have a dog tied up my back.'

A Northern Ireland family in a Devon boarding house left the remainder of the English-speaking guests wondering what communication was all about by addressing to each other such queries as, 'Are ye headin' out?' and by being sometimes asked, 'Have you been here previous?'

It was no help in clearing the air when the question was put to a guest from Macclesfield, 'Are you readin' that paper you're sittin on?'

'Thon pijuns breed like black taxis.'

Few things reveal more effectively the kind of person you are than your speech; we place people by the way they talk. How an Ulsterwoman speaks betrays her character more revealingly than her dress or her looks.

Listen to the owner of a budgerigar affectionately discussing her pet: 'It flies round the room as happy as Larry. It settles on top of the foam and sits there for ires preenin' its wee self an' chitterin' away.'

The words conjure up a picture of the speaker which would not be at all possible if you were merely to see her.

Take the incident in one of Belfast's troubled areas. A bus has been hi-jacked by a gang of youths and set on fire. Children are singing and dancing gleefully round it. A woman passing the spot with a friend comments, 'Ach but isn't is gran' to see the wee childer laughin'? It does yer heart good to see themselves enjoyin' themselves.'

Hear the Shankill Road housewife denouncing a pet dog, 'It just lives for barkin' and fightin'. Just listen to it. It's out there at the back barkin' away at everybody an' nobody there.'

The unexpected phrase bobbing up from nowhere makes it a reward to be around when an Ulsterwoman speaks.

One was complaining bitterly of the nuisance caused by the extensive pigeon loft of the man next door.

'Thon pijuns is desperate,' she said. 'Flyin' round all day. Nivver at rest. An' ye can't put out the washin' for them. There's that many of them. Sure they breed like black taxis so they do.'

Anyone who has seen the black taxis of Belfast out in strength during rush hour will appreciate the aptness of the simile.

The lady who confessed that she had 'got beyond herself' and become over-boisterous during a party is paralleled by the one who said she was 'beside herself'.

Certainly it would be hard to come by the Ulsterwoman who would question the statement that confession is good for the soul.

'I'm awful glad a run intil you,' said a woman to a friend in a super-market. 'D'ye mine what a toul ye? To tell ye the truth it was all a pack av lies.'

You will hear the explanation, 'I can stummick him but I can't stand her,' which ranks in frankness with the comment, 'That woman next door would take the milk outa your tea.'

A dedicated attention to detail is paid in the instruction given by a house-wife to her family as she left on an unexpected errand, 'I'll be back in ten minutes. Don't forget to put the teapot on in about half-an-hour.'

The lady summed up a Mediterranean holiday in a few terse words, 'Ach it was all right but the sea was boggin'.'

She had much the same touch as the woman who told a friend, 'I saw him dancin' in the middle of the flure with a beard.'

The mind boggles at the complications many Ulsterwomen introduce when they have something to say, no matter how simple.

'Her husband's cousin's daughter's son married his second cousin and went to live with an uncle and aunt on his father's side.'

'He said he got browned aff waitin' on a red bus and just tuk a black taxi.'

'Them fellas workin' on that buildin' site facin' us. They're nivver done finishin' early.'

'It was only last night I knew it was the day.'

'Have you noticed that there's a quare drap in the nights?'

'It's a pity of her. She's a wee orphand.'

'D'ye know this, I'm sick of this bad coal I'm gettin'. I declare I carry out more than I bring in.'

A woman looking at a family snap was heard to comment, 'That wee child. He'd be awful like your morr if he didn't look so much like your farr.'

Unexpected too, is the philosophy indicated by the conversation sparked off by a stuffed dog on show in a second-hand store.

'Ach, the poor wee thing,' a woman customer said to her companion. 'I suppose everybody belongin' to it is dead and gone.'

'Aye, indeed,' agreed her companion, 'an' the dog's still there.'

'Right enough,' was the sad comment.

There is a basic, down to earth homeliness about the way an Ulsterwoman will put things that has something in common with that to be found among Dublin women.

A Shankill Road woman summed up the size of the small house at the seaside she had rented for the summer in the words, 'It's that wee you could sit on the toilet and pay the milkman at the front door.'

This makes an interesting comparison with the comment of the Dublin woman who was taking her pet dog for a walk in the park.

'I'm getting tired of this animal of mine,' she complained. 'It keeps sniffing round the other dogs that much that it makes me ashamed. The way it gets on — I feel that embarrassed.'

'I wouldn't let that worry you too much,' said her friend. 'After all they're only human.'

But when it comes to the really biting comment the ladies reign supreme.

A Co Down woman summed up her feelings about an acquaintance like this, 'If she thinks I'll speak to her again she has another think coming. If she holds her hand over her backside she'll have a handful before I open my mouth to her.'

Largely because of the womenfolk the variations on the *See Me, See Her?* theme continue to flourish. Examples worth recording include —

'See me? I have no teeth but begod I have very willing gums.'

'See her? She has legs like shovel shafts and no man wants her.'

'See her? She has a mouthful of raisins.'

'See her? She's going baldy for a hair dryer for her birthday.'

'See her? I wouldn't say she can't keep a secret. It's not that she tells everybody. Just them that don't know it.'

'See her? She has as many wrinkles on her face as would hold a fortnight's rain.'

'See her? When she tells you you're looking well she makes you feel as if she can hardly believe her eyes.'

'See him? Every time I set eyes on him he's miraculously dressed.'

'See him? He can't stand work. If his next door neighbour was in bed with the cold he'd stay out in sympathy.'

'See him? He has a quare oul mouth for coolin' broth.'

'See him? The only thing that fella would give you is the hump.'

'See him? I wudden take his haun if I was drownin'.'

'See him? You could fry the pan on that fella's overalls.'

'See him? He's that iggerant he thinks John Bunyan was a charapadist.'

The statement 'See me? Without my glasses,' is a comment that speaks for itself.

'There's a man rapping the door wi' a beard.'

Much of the pattern of Ulster speech is firmly established during childhood.

What children hear in the family circle is so constantly in ill-accord with the principles taught at school that it is not surprising that the influence of the home plays an important part in their use of language.

How could a child possibly make the adjustment when he hears his mother lament, 'Luck at this wee lad of mine. He has my head turned. I bought him a new school blazer and he wouldn't wear it. If I hadn't got it for him it would never have been aff his back.'

A lost Belfast younger defied all efforts by police to establish her identity. In desperation the officer asked, 'What does your mummy call your daddy?'

'She doesn't call him anything,' was the reply. 'She likes him.'

And few Ulster parents would think of correcting the small boy who told them, 'There's a funny man rapping the door wi' a beard.'

A boy asked his next door neighbour, 'Can I have the lend of your saw? My farr wants to make a dog box for my rabbit.'

Doubtless he had heard his mother make the statement, 'I'm going down to the shop for a cardboard tin of biscuits.'

And it is quite feasible that the same source was the inspiration for the claim, 'My wee girl is awful good at recimitations.'

Children who hear grown-ups make such statements as, 'I keep telling my wee girl to eat her dinner but it just goes in one ear and out the other,' are bound to be influenced by this approach to speech.

It is a fair guess that it had a lot to do with the remark of the youngster, watching a poorly attended football match on television, 'Look at all the people that aren't there.'

A boy found by his mother staring into the bathroom mirror with intense concentration was asked what he was doing and replied gravely, 'You told me to watch myself.'

A little girl received this extraordinary command from her mother, 'Go out into the garden and play yourself. And if I look out and you're not there I'll bring you in.'

The cold, irresistible logic of the child mind can sometimes be disconcerting to their elders.

'I'm going to have to read the Riot Act to you two,' a mother warned her boisterous children.

'Good,' cried one of them. 'Come and we'll get into our pyjamas. Mummy's going to read to us.'

A teacher impatiently asked one of her pupils, 'Surely you know what minus means?'

'Aren't they the people who dig coal?' she was asked.

Another youngster was in tears at school because the family's pet cat had died.

'I didn't cry my eyes out when my grandmother died last week,' said the teacher in an effort to console her.

'But you didn't have her from a kitten,' retorted the sobbing infant.

A Ballymena child is credited with a triumph of sorts when the class was given an arithmetic test by a new teacher.

She asked them to give her a number. One boy said '23'. The teacher wrote '32' on the blackboard, and asked for another number.

A pupil suggested '15' and '51' appeared.

A further number was asked for and a boy at the back of the class put up his hand and said, '33 and see what ye can dae with that.'

Ulster children will understand clearly what is meant when they are rebuked, 'Don't give me any of your owl lip. Do as you are bid.'

Not always, however, are the younger generation unaware of the fact that there are precepts in speech which should be observed.

A Belfast boy was heard telling a companion, 'It's not yousens. It's youse.'

Similarly a little girl received the rebuke from a schoolmate, 'You keep saying "a hennae". That's wrong. It should be "a hae noan".'

The fact remains that should a Northern Ireland child go astray in any other community he faces problems in making himself understood.

How could it be otherwise if he is asked his name and replies 'Sarry'? In how many cases would it be appreciated that he answers to 'Harry'?

And on this subject, Ulster parents need to exercise caution in their selection for their brand-new offspring because of the tendency in Norn Iron to mangle the most inoffensive and pretty names. An extreme example cropped up in a conversation between an Ulster mother and a visitor from England in which the fond parent regaled her companion with tales of her little daughter, Antnet. The visitor marvelled politely at the child's accomplishments and then inquired how she had come by her unusual name.

'Well,' explained the happy mother, 'we just call her that for short. Her full name is M'ree Antnet — you know, after the French queen who got herself gelatined.'

'Ah'd luck like somethin' come outa the grave for a smoak.'

In Ulster the doctor's waiting room is looked on as an institution designed to facilitate confession at its most uninhibited. It is an accepted setting for the exchange of revelations of complete intimacy, a place to tell all and hear everything.

There are no secrets among those waiting to see the doctor, which is a factor that can have its own therapeutic value. The waiting room is often as important to the sufferer as the surgery itself.

Its status was made clear in the rebuke earned by the woman who went to the length of grumbling that she had had much too protracted a wait to see the doctor.

'But sure it's part of the cure,' she was told.

Also reflecting a common attitude to the waiting room is the remark, 'I suppose I could be a lot worse. Still I only go for the crack.'

Not usual, however, was the complaint of the patient who felt she could have spent her time more profitably, 'What's keeping the doctor so long? He should know I'm not here for the good of my health.'

A woman arriving late offered this explanation to the others. 'I was redd up early and I feel all right but I thought I'd come down to the doctor anyway. You never know what's wrong with you these days and it passes an hour.'

The value of the surgery as a haunt of the unwell was also underlined by a comment on the absence of one of the regulars, 'She hasn't been here this wheen o' weeks now. There must be somethin' wrong with the poor woman. *Maybe she's not well.*'

The degree to which it is a haven of comfort is reflected in the words of the Co Antrim woman who said, 'I feel bravely but I thought the doctor might see something I can't find.'

One waiting-room exchange took this form:

'And how are ye gettin' on?'

'Ach nat so well. I hadda come the day to get some of the tablets he give me but I don't think they're doin' much good.'

'Ach well sure it takes ye outa the house for an hour.'

The surgery is a place where 'How are you feeling?' is asked automatically for the atmosphere is that of a club. Sometimes to put the question is like throwing down the gauntlet, challenging you to reveal just how close you might be to death's door.

'Some days I feel ninety,' will come the revelation. 'Others I just feel myself.'

One woman exclaimed, 'I was that far through I went upstairs and threw myself down.'

One reply introduced its own element of drama, 'Ach I was awful bad a coupla weeks ago there. I thought it was curtains. Even when the dog came inta the room it had its tail down.'

Answers can take the form of a taciturn 'Mallrite' (and the more taciturn the acknowledgment the worse could be the condition) or they can run to 'Me? Sure I was throwin' aff buckets the whole night.'

Sometimes there will be the admission 'I'll be all right when I'm a bit better' but the unusual inevitably rears its head, as in the case of the woman who 'disallocated' her neck, and the Ballymena housewife who said her husband was having terrible trouble with his 'vowels'.

One patient went home after a consultation convinced that she had a 'slipped discus'.

She had something in common, perhaps, with the Belfastwoman who lamented, 'Them suppositories leave an awful bad taste in your mouth.'

Medical men in Ulster must always be on their toes; the sharp retort is forever threatening. A doctor told a patient, 'I'll drop in and see you in the morning,' and was promptly asked, 'You'll see me, doctor, but will I see you?'

Exchanging details about one's symptoms sometimes produces unusual admissions.

'When a cough a feel as if the oul chest's full av broken glass,' a woman said. 'Is that the way you feel?'

'No,' was the firm reply. 'It's more like trying to cough with an owl whin bush caught in my thrapple.'

A Co Armagh woman, recovering from an illness, tried to explain to a friend why she was bareheaded, even in February. 'A hae ma hat in ma beg but a didnae pit it on for ah'd luck like somethin' come outa the grave for a smoak.'

A hospital patient who was asked how she was feeling replied, 'Not so hot,' and was immediately brought another blanket.

A woman explained to a friend, 'Know what am' goin' till tell ye?

There's a spring av watter runnin' outa ma head like Niagra Falls.'

'God help me,' came the answer. 'My tap's leakin' too. But sure we may be thankful we're here for wan nivver knows where you're goin' these days, even on the bus.'

There is a philosophy of its own about the reflection of the Newry woman, 'When I take the flu it always goes to my head and when it takes the feet from under me a hafta go an' lie down.'

'My arm's that stiff I can't bent it straight,' lamented one woman. Another grumbled, 'A fell on the heel of ma han'.'

Legs, fingers, arms, heads, feet — all seem to acquire a personality of their own in the waiting room.

'Your finger's beelin'. You'll hafta ast the dactar to let it out.'

'A'm havin' awful trouble with this left-hand fut of mine.'

'I towl the dactar my stummick was bad and I cudden get rid of it and he said he didden think anybody wud want it.'

'I ast him if he cud give me somethin' to bring my leg to a head.'

Another way of indicating that you find yourself, so to speak, out on a limb, runs 'Funny enough I cudden get intil the car with my legs.'

'I was in bed with my legs,' was a lament which brought the understanding response, 'Me. I just dread goin' to bed with my legs.'

A heart cry ran, 'Ah've lived with this owl leg av mine for the last seven years.'

One waiting room gathering nodded sympathetically when a new arrival said, 'I cudden do a thing all week. My corn hasn't stapped leppin'.'

A mother warned her small son as he set off with his new skateboard, 'Now don't come runnin' home to me with a broken leg.'

Digestive problems are a constant topic of conversation, outside as well as inside the waiting room.

A piece of advice which calls for a close knowledge of Ulster speech ran, 'Talk about prunes. Them figs is the quare mark.'

It serves to emphasize the communication gap underlined in the words of an Ulsterwoman after a visit to Yorkshire.

'Them people don't understand plain English,' she announced. 'I said to a woman, "Missus, you're quare an' well mended", and she didn't know what I was talkin' about.'

Ulster's GPs must be prepared at all times to handle strange situations. They are required to keep a straight face when confronted with such appeals as, 'Cud ye help me, doctor? It's my man's after-shave. It makes me sick to my stummick.'

'The rain's comin' down in torments.'

Being such a strongly agricultural community the weather figures largely as a topic of conversation in Ulster. It is a safe bet that as a subject it has an edge on politics.

Whether it is wet or dry, cold or warm, Ulster people feel compelled to make a comment about it.

'That's awful like a mornin' that was out all night' is as much a remark about the climate as a reflection of a feeling of gloom.

The man who said, 'The wine was that strong I had to face it with my back,' was not admitting that he had over-indulged. His complaint was about the strong wind.

You will be told, 'That's a desperate day,' or, 'If it rains like this till the marra it'll be damp all night.'

As her husband was having breakfast a Belfastwoman looked out of the window and commented, 'I wouldn't send a dog out on a day like that,' then added in the same breath, 'It's time you were away to your work.'

I have heard the comment, 'Look at that rain. It's coming down in torments.'

Another weather exchange ran, 'It was hard to hold your feet this morning.'

'Aye indeed,' came the reply, 'for there I was up to my haughs in snow.'

During a heavy shower I was told, 'It's not half coming down,' and then came the disclosure, 'Sure we never got through the dure all day yesterday. What's the weather coming to?'

If someone says, 'That's great wire' it is not advisable to get the idea that a barbed wire fence is being praised. A tribute to the day is intended.

An Ulster visitor to New York was asked where she had been and explained, 'Ach a had a notion to take a wee dander roun' the shops till see if a cud fine something for me da's birthday. But a hardly got up yonder when it started till spit and before ye knew the rain wasn't even taking time to come down and me a dirty walker. I got japped all the way up. Serves me right for goin' out in me figure.'

If you are told 'It's only a wee shar' you can be sure that only a mild drizzle has to be faced, while an interesting piece of weather lore lies behind the statement by a farm worker, 'That train whistle is far too clear for my likin'.'

A Belfast breadserver knew better than to do no more than nod in resigned agreement when serving a customer in a downpour.

'Isn't it cowl and wet,' she said to him. 'It's well there's nobody out in it.'

'He can wallace with anybody so he can.'

Ulstermen are not noted for flights of romantic fancy. When they go a-wooing they keep their emotions under firm control. Their relations with the opposite sex are not allowed to get out of hand. A woman must be kept in her place.

Advances achieved by Women's Lib have not completely passed Northern Ireland by, save perhaps in country districts, yet the man seen pushing a pram can still be sure of drawing curious glances, not necessarily chauvinistic ones.

Domestically women make all the sounds of firmly ruling the roost.

A Banbridge woman replied to an inquiry about her husband's health by explaining, 'He's all right only it takes him a quare while to pull himself together in the mornings.'

As a rule the ladies seem to think it is expected of them to say things about their husbands that indicate rather less than contempt.

The complaint, 'I'm sick to my stummick luckin' at him sittin' there with a face like a cowl poultice,' is not uncommon.

Nor is the indictment, 'As soon as he gets intil the house he's stuck in front of the telly and nivver spakes till the Queen. I wudden mine only he's asleep all the time.'

But compliments can also be encountered. 'Every Sunday morning in life John brings me up a cup of tea in bed. There's not many like him for he has a terrible melody, the sowl. Still it doesn't stap him dancin'. He can wallace with anybody so he can.'

One husband told his wife, 'There was an awful storm during the night. Thunder and lightning and rain. It was terrible.'

'Why didn't you waken me?' she demanded. 'You know I can't sleep a wink when there's lightning.'

A wife confided to a friend, 'I asked him if his knee hurt and he said "No, only when I want it." Men!'

A husband grumbled about the dust on the bedroom mirror. 'I could write my name on it,' he complained.

'Write it oftener, then,' he was told, 'and it won't need dusting.'

A not uncommon approach to married life is said to have been demonstrated by the Co Fermanagh couple who visited the minister to make arrangements for their wedding. His house was reached by a long, narrow lane and when they were ushered in and had waited for some little time he eventually arrived, all set to take the necessary details.

Unnerved by the long wait, however, the prospective groom greeted him with the words, 'Nivver borr. I've tuck a scunner at her. It's all aff,' and stalked out.

Some weeks later, their differences apparently healed, the couple paid a second visit to the parsonage. Again the cleric kept them waiting but when he entered the room it was the girl this time who announced, 'Ach I'm not going to go through with it. It's me that's taken a scunner at him.'

After the lapse of another few weeks they made a third appointment to see the cleric but as they approached the house he opened the window and called out, 'You needn't bother your heads coming any further. I've taken a scunner at the pair of you.'

I am assured that at a wedding in a Co Antrim church the bridegroom, a sailor, when asked, 'Will thou take this woman?' kept answering in seafaring style, 'Aye, aye sir.'

'But you must say "I will",' he was reminded. 'Nothing else will do.' Once more the question was put.

Again he answered, 'Aye, aye sir.'

Annoyed, the minister threatened to stop the ceremony if the proper response was not forthcoming.

'Look, mister,' the bride exclaimed anxiously. 'If you don't quit badgering him you'll have him saying "I won't" in a minute.'

A man involved in a long and persistent courtship was asked why he didn't marry the girl.

'She never asked me,' was his reply.

His approach was not unlike that of the young man who took the object of his affections on a bus run to Bangor. During a stroll round the resort they stopped at a shop window.

'Isn't that nice chocolate,' he said. 'You should go in a buy yourself a bar.'

The girl did so and when she got home told her mother what had happened. She was dumbfounded at such meanness. She asked if he had paid the girl's bus fare and was told he had.

Angrily she gave the girl the money and told her to take it back to him at once.

When the young woman got to the house her suitor was in bed but finally responded to her knocking.

Told he was being paid back the money he had spent on their outing he said, 'Thanks very much but sure you shouldn't have bothered your head. It would have done all right at the week end.'

'I wouldn't warm to him even if we were to be cremated together.'

In a manner of speaking the wake is a dying custom in Ulster. Sitting round the coffin well into the small hours drinking endless toasts to the corpse is no longer considered an essential last tribute. An impressive turn out of mourners matters more than being able to keep a wake going for forty-eight hours.

Nevertheless it has not been entirely abolished, even if it has ceased to be so prolonged. It continues to be an excuse for 'one for the road', otherwise 'a noggin' to send the departed convivially on his way.

To visit a house where there has been a bereavement is sure to give rise to problems for those who don't speak the language.

It is not easy, for example, for anyone not in the know to show understanding when a valedictory takes this form, 'She hadn't much of a life, the poor sowl, but I'm sure she's the happy woman now she has her head happed.'

Solemnly it was said of a plumber who suffered a fatal heart attack while repairing a faulty cistern, 'Sure he wasn't at himself for a whole week before it happened.'

At a Co Antrim wake a mourner summed up her conception of a contented hereafter by the statement, 'If iver I die, and I hope I won't, I'd like to be buried near the railway line for I always love to hear the trains goin' by.'

This was how another woman voiced her feelings about a relative who had passed on: 'He was the nicest corp I saw for many's a long day. Did you know they had him embezzled? They said he was six and a half feet tall but he was a quare nice wee man.'

A whispered indictment heard at a wake in North Down was, 'I nivver thought much of him. To tell you the truth I wouldn't warm to him even if we were to be cremated together.'

A Co Antrim farmer, when given the news of his brother's sudden death, was told, 'He washed and shaved and took a hearty breakfast before he set off for the fair he was fated never to reach. Wasn't it sad?'

'Ah well,' was the resigned comment. 'He didnae dee with a dirty face or an empty stummick.'

Funeral costs are a frequent source of concern in country districts. There is a constant struggle between a no-expense-spared burial and a more prudent approach to the last rites.

In a discussion about the type of shroud proposed for her late husband the widow protested at the price quoted by the undertaker.

'If I shopped around a bit I'm sure I could get one for half that,' she objected.

'Maybe,' she was told, 'but woman dear the material wouldn't be in it. Sure the corpse would have his knees through it in a week. Ye wouldn't want that, would ye?'

When asked by an undertaker if she would like one of the latest styles in shrouds for her aged brother a woman answered, 'A plain one will do him rightly. He won't get much wear out of it anyway.'

When it comes to epitaphs it is difficult to beat this example from a country area of Co Armagh. There had been a mix-up over the funeral arrangements and the cortège had a long wait.

'Him,' said one of the mourners about the deceased. 'Ach, when he was livin' I always said he'd miss his own funeral. Sure his da used to call him "owl time enough".'

A woman with a teenage daughter almost as tall as herself asked in a dress shop for 'something to suit the wee girl'.

After showing her everything feasible without success the assistant finally asked, 'Just what sort of dress do you mind in mind, missus?'

'It's for her uncle's weddin',' came the reply, 'but I would like to get something that would pass her at her granda's funeral for he's been laid aside this good while now.'

It sounds like a contradiction in terms but none is intended when someone says, 'Funny enough, he died the same day as his wife.'

A element of its own was introduced at a Co Londonderry wake. The deceased lady had a reputation for strength of will; a woman who usually had her own way. During the proceedings a thunderstorm developed and a blinding flash of lightning was followed by a loud clap of thunder.

'Dear help them up there,' murmured a mourner with feeling. 'She must have arrived.'

It was at a wake for a Shankill Road woman, also noted for her firmness of character, that someone said, 'Ach, she's gettin' her last wish. She always wanted to lie in Dundonald Cemetery. She said it was awful well kept.'

'I heard her say that myself,' agreed a hearer. 'In fact she towl me once she wouldn't be caught dead in Carnmoney.'

Wakes can vary according to the interests of the deceased. One of them, intended to mark the passing of a well-known Lambeg drummer, brought its own special note.

Lambegs, of course, are known less for tunefulness than for noise. This did not deter the man's friends from staging what they considered an

'A plain one will do him rightly. He won't get much wear out of it anyway.'

appropriate farewell. They held the wake in the local Orange Hall, from which the dead man had often set out, drum-sticks flailing.

The fact that above the thunder of the drums played by the mourners no one could hear a word of regret at his passing did not matter. Their tribute had been paid.

This was also the motive underlying the comment of the Tyrone farmer who was 'paying his last respects' at the wake of a neighbour. As he stood looking down at the corpse he said to the dead man's son, 'I never saw a man went to hell like your father.'

What he wanted to convey was the extent to which the deceased had suffered from failing health. The son understood. A stranger wouldn't have had the same comprehension.

'He's no fren. That fella's a Baptist.'

By the nature of things religion is taken seriously in Ulster. Visitors soon discover that a sermon is no laughing matter.

Pastor and priest are important local figures, with this distinction: while Catholics think their clergy can do no wrong, many Protestants are convinced that if the minister is a paragon it is only a matter of time before his flaws come to light.

When the minister calls at the house the Protestant will immediately turn down the sound on his television set. If the priest calls the Catholic will mutter to himself 'Damn it' and dutifully switch the set off.

An indication of the obsession with religion is reflected in the bewildering experience of a visiting cleric who was stopped in the street in an Ulster town by two churchgoers. As they chatted one of them waved to someone on the other side of the street.

'Who's that?' his companion asked, 'Is he a fren?'

'Him? He's no fren,' was the prompt reply. 'That fella's a Baptist.'

A Presbyterian elder, discussing a prospective new incumbent, gave his verdict thus, 'That's the man for me. He's nice and well educated. I listened to his sermon and I cudden understand a word he said from I went in till I went out.'

A minister on his return from a holiday asked a parishioner how how young assistant had managed during his absence.

'He was all right, I suppose,' was the reply, 'but to tell ye the truth I'd far rather listen to yourself talkin' in your own owl ignorant way.'

It is not always advisable for a pastor to probe too deeply into the likes and dislikes of his flock.

A new cleric asked a member of his parish to be frank. 'Tell me,' he inquired, 'just what sort of a congregation is this? Are they good churchgoers?'

'Weel, so far as I have seen,' was the grave reply, 'there's only two Christians among the lot of them — the wife and myself. And begod sometimes I have my doubts about her.'

One parishioner, troubled with a nagging wife, asked the minister if he would have a word with her. The cleric was reluctant to interfere but finally agreed to see what he could do to help.

He duly went to the house and was met by the husband who asked him if he would mind waiting outside for a moment or two.

'Just stand there for a wee tick,' was the request. 'Wait till I go in and get her started. You'll see for yourself what she's like.'

A minister who engaged a farm labourer to work a field attached to the manse decided to check on the progress he was making. He found the man taking his ease, the horses resting, little of the work accomplished.

'I know the horses have to have a breather,' he said, 'but couldn't you take the clippers and be trimming the hedge when they're resting?'

'Aye,' said the labourer drily. 'Maybe. But many's the time I've thought if you had a dish of taties in the pulpit on Sunday you could be peelin' them while the people are singin'.'

A church meeting attracted only a small attendance because it had been brought forward a day at short notice.

When the minister voiced disappointment at the poor gathering a member of the audience jumped to his feet and declared, 'There would hav been plenty here the night if the meeting had been held tomorrow as originally planned.'

In a Co Down village a resident was asked, 'Have you been spakin' to the new minister's wife yet?'

'A heven't.'

'Ach ye needn't be feeared,' was the advice. 'Sure she'd spake to anybody.'

There could not have been a more handsome tribute.

'You could be peelin' them while the people are singin'.'

'She was lovely in her dynamite earrings.'

A facility for coining a makeshift substitute for a word which has eluded the memory comes as second nature in Ulster. Mrs Malaprop's creator would have found it a place flowing over with examples of her touch.

A Belfastwoman, grumbling about her husband's insistence on salads, summed up his enthusiasm for greens with the comment, 'Ach but he's odd. He just lives for robot food.'

An assistant in a furniture store took it in his stride when faced with the request, 'Cud I hev a wee luck at yir Devon beds?'

It is fairly common for council tenants to complain of the trouble caused by condescension but one tenant went even further. 'The condemnation wud break yir heart,' she insisted.

As a rule gardeners are not people who die young. One of them provided his own proof by the statement, 'Ye cud say I was an octogeranium.'

Violence has made its own contribution to the vernacular in Northern Ireland. Unfortunately it is an ever-lengthening one.

It was said of a soldier on riot duty, 'He was stannin' there pointin' his harmalot rifle intil the air.'

It is interesting to picture the police officer involved in a hoax bomb scare, 'He had his haun on his Wembley revolver so he had.'

And it offers an uneasy prospect to picture the radiant bride of whom it was said, 'Ach but she lucked lovely in her dynamite earrings.'

A Belfast printing firm taking an order for wedding invitations was firmly instructed, 'Put plenty of astericks on them. Astericks luck awful well.'

A woman complaining about a wall covered with the inevitable scribbling said, 'Isn't it terrible to see all that gravity?'

'Ach sure it's all them ersel sprays,' her companion answered. 'The shaps shudden't be allowed to sell them.'

Which has similarities with the remark of the Belfast housewife about her husband, 'Innver since he gat that new job his timekeeping has been terrible erotic.'

Sometimes the word in the speaker's mind is not easily grasped. When a Co Fermanagh man's two children had a narrow escape in a car crash he remarked thankfully, 'They could have been sitting there like two parables for the rest of their days.'

Social security benefits have almost developed a vocabulary of their own.

Variations of the real thing are now so commonplace that they sometimes take the place of the original, even in official circles.

A woman making a claim for infidelity benefit almost made it seem that she was being deprived of her rights when asked if she didn't mean invalidity benefit.

A claimant for a mobility allowance was more philosophical, 'Ability allowance, nobility allowance,' she announced. 'I don't care what you call it so long as I get it.'

There are other arenas where the absence of the precise word makes for confusion, as was the case with the Co Armagh woman describing a neighbour's adoration of his young wife, 'He thinks a quare lot of her. He even give her a gold plastic purse for their weddin' anniversary.'

The man whose eyes were said to have been 'double glazed' after a rather boisterous celebration earns its own special niche. So does the soccer player whose team was 'delegated to the fourth division' and the 'printer who ran 100 yards in ten seconds.'

It is an unexpected tribute to a holiday in the Spanish sun to hear the boast 'We were able to sit out on the vivanda all day.'

I would have my doubts that the woman who complained of a neighbour, 'She was shouting epitaphs at me' was aware that Sheridan had beaten her to it. It would make little difference. She would be happy that she had made her point.

A boarding-house guest caused some bewilderment when she confessed to the landlady that she was 'terrible fond of cock-a-doodle soup.' It took a little thought for it to be worked out that cock-a-leekie was meant.

Certainly most listeners would have to think twice before getting the hang of the statement credited to a Co Londonderry woman, 'I got two unanimous letters last week. I'm goin' to the police.'

The way in which out of the ordinary requests made to shopkeepers are met without turning a hair is one aspect of the Province's life-style with its own special qualities.

It calls for a considerable degree of tact to look as if it is routine, all in the day's work, to cope with such requests as:

'What's the price of your colour gas heaters?'

'I would like to have a look at some of them fari suits.'

'How much would a humble drier cost?'

'I have a suit I want reupholstered.'

'We're gettin' our curtains fixed. Cud I see some of yir pelvis?'

'Are them wash-dishers very dear?'

'I want a jar of after-shave potion for himself.'

'We're goin' to do up the kitchen. Could I have a cuppla tins of Durex paint?'

'We're aff to Majorca next week. Cud I see some sandglasses?'

'I want some incidental powder for my man's teeth.'

'They're goin' made about coffee in our house. I'd like to see one of them copulators.'

'You'll be all right in the morning if you stay in bed till dinner time.'

A report in the *Guardian* newspaper on the quality of Northern Ireland local radio programmes concluded with the words, 'In stark contrast to the uncompromising middle-class accents of BBC Radio Ulster, Downtown Radio is sometimes so indigenous that it is incomprehensible to the outsider.'

The writer was clearly conscious that this lack of understanding emphasised the degree to which he felt himself to be an alien, a stranger in a strange land.

If it is a fact that the treatment often given to the English language in Ulster could hardly be described as respectful it still produces singular results, as I have surely shown. The outsider who finds it so much beyond his grasp misses a great deal.

Apart from such malpractices as deliberately leaving the 'u' out of laundry, and calling a cow a 'coo', the combination of what is said and how it is uttered makes for many of the complications.

A woman in a bus told her companion 'I saw the dacter last week and he said I'd be all right in the mornin' provided I lay in bed till dinner time. What d'ye think the man meant?'

In a shopping queue a woman was told, 'That's a nice wee boy you have with you.'

She replied, 'D'ye know this? When I have him sittin' on my knee and I see the back of his head it's just like his da luckin' at me.'

It was pouring as two women came out of church and one was heard to say 'Did you ivver see such heavy rain?'

'No,' was the reply. 'Nivver. It makes ye wonder where it all comes from. I lucked this mornin' an' it was pourin' down my back.'

Not immediately obvious is the meaning of the comment about a prosperous neighbour, 'She's on the pig's back now. Sure her house is coming down.'

It would be unwise to assume that the building had been condemned. What was meant was that it was filled to overflowing with new furniture, new carpets, new ornaments, and a host of other examples of domestic well-being.

When two Ulster holidaymakers were sightseeing among the ruins of Florence one called her companion's attention to a spot they were passing and wondered what it was.

'Ach, it's only one of them owl ghettoes,' she was told impatiently.

It had been a wet morning but in the afternoon the sun came out and was blazing down when a bus passenger said to the woman beside her, 'You wudden think it was the same day as we come up.'

A woman who did cleaning work for an elderly lady who kept half a dozen cats for company decided to give up the job. 'I cudden stick them beely-johns any longer,' she said. 'No matter what I said to them they just sat an' lucked at me.'

A husband who had been taking a few days holiday awoke on the first morning of his break at his usual time of 6.30 am. He lay in thought for some moments before turning to his wife and saying, 'I think I'll go downstairs and make a drop of tea before I get up.'

A tendency to ask pointless questions is basic to the Ulster character.

A girl got herself locked in a factory toilet which had just been fitted with a new lock. When she was eventually freed she asked a colleague if she hadn't heard her calls for help.

'No,' was the reply. 'Did you get out all right?'

But the gift for the unusual metaphor is also instinctive.

It was said of a girl who was inordinately thin, 'She has herself killed with them slimmin' tablets. She must be the thinnest woman in the town.'

'I wouldn't say that,' came the reply. 'The new teacher in the girls' school is as thin as two of her.'

A man sympathising with a friend over the death of a relative commented 'It was very sudden.'

'It was that,' came the reply. 'He went quicker than the clap of a duck's wing.'

Who could disdain a manner of speaking in which such imagery comes as second nature?

'Come on on in for a wee skelly.'

Suggestions are made from time to time that public notices in Ulster would meet with a better response if put into Norn Iron instead of the more formal phrasing normally used.

It is urged that if this were done they could be more readily appreciated by the natives, even if the visitor might not be so fortunate. Visitors, it is felt, could be given a fool's pardon.

There are arguments, for example, in favour of the idiomatic version of 'Please wait until the bus stops,' which would run 'Stan' yer groun' till it pulls up.'

This, in fact, is rather more effective if spoken, for usually in Ulster 'pull' is made to rhyme with 'dull' or 'bull'.

It is possible that trade would be helped if a shop displayed the invitation 'Come on on in for a wee skelly' rather than 'Come in and look around'.

There is a directness about 'Shut yer bake' as a substitute for the more genteel 'Silence please', and 'Nathin' on tick' as an alternative to 'Please do not ask for credit as a denial often offends'.

The familiar 'Keep off the verge' acquires a fresh flavour if turned into 'Mine where yer goin'.' It would be an interesting experiment to see which proved the more effective.

Certainly if directness really produced results then 'Nick yer fegs' would win hands down over 'No smoking', and 'Our shop's stickin' out' would be superior to 'The best store in town'.

'Trespassers prosecuted' has had a long run. It is a nice question if the time has come to vary it and warn 'Nobody let in here or they'll get their name tuck.' To get your name taken in Ulster is an experience to be dreaded.

'Use ordure' would shock the average visitor beyond belief if unaware that it meant 'Use other door'. 'Pull the door till' as a revised version of 'Please close the door' might also leave the uninformed in the dark.

A fruitshop notice 'Don't fissel with the greens' would be self-explanatory in most cases. Outsiders, however, might not instantly grasp that it was an injunction not to handle them.

But the confusion apt to be caused to tourists encountering 'Only ijits don't use this road' rather than 'This way' make it clear that the vernacular can have certain drawbacks.

'No matter what it is if ye cook it he'll ate it.'

Ulster preferences in food are basically on the simple side. It is not a region noted for its epicures, or as a paradise for the gourmet.

The general attitude is summed up by the Co Down man who had been entertained to a considerable meal of three fried eggs, several rashers of bacon, fried soda galore, and a number of slices of bread and butter as well as cake. When he finished his fourth cup of tea he was heard to murmur as he pushed it away from him, 'That was a nice wee drap of tea.'

The guest who announced, 'I can't ate with my teeth' had her own special problem, one which did not apply to the husband of whom it was said, 'No matter what it is, if ye cook it he'll ate it.'

The invitation, 'Could ye face a brown egg?' would stump the average visitor, just as it would make him raise his eyebrows to hear the statement, 'My Aunt Aggie always does her own bakin'. She always said the pirty oaten left her nails nice and clean.'

One long-suffering wife summed up her tribulations in the lament, 'That oul lad of mine, ye cudden fill him. No sooner has he finished one meal but he asts what time's the next one.'

If nothing else, Ulster people are connoisseurs when it comes to a cup of tea.

As one was being poured out for her, a visitor exclaimed, 'Just give me what you would know for I've been suppin' it all mornin'.'

There is a note of refinement about the claim, 'We would never make a cup of tea without boiling the water first. We're very particular.'

A hearty appetite was indicated by the small boy who was asked how he had enjoyed a party and replied, 'Well I was the last yin to quit atin' forby them yins that gaed oot the tay an' wee buns.'

Nobody but an Ulsterman would have called out as he walked into an empty English cafe, 'How's the tay howlin' out?'

I suspect that Yorkshire and other areas have their own versions of the request made by a small boy in a Belfast shop, 'Givvus a loaf and two toilet rolls for m'da's tea.'

One unexpected admission ran, 'I love the owl orange now and then.' Doubtless the same speaker was responsible for the complaint heard in a greengrocer's, 'Oranges! Nobody wud call them oranges. Sure ye cud bulk marleys with them.'

The lady who said, 'I just love a cuppa tay in a bowel' is a rarity nowadays and not often encountered is the confession, 'I never take burr an' jam at the same time. I like them both right enough but not togerr.'

This brought the reply, 'Isn't that funny now? Seein' you're fond of them both aren't you powerful sore on the bread?'

Reflecting the simple tastes that are so often the rule is the dialogue overheard in Belfast shipyard.

'Did you get a fish supper for your dinner the day?' a man asked.

'Naw,' said his workmate. 'Thisus the piece the morr made up. There's a fog feed of tin beef in it forby a brave lock of them water biscuits but she knows rightly I'd rar have dip at my dinner hour.'

The wee shap.

Once a Belfastwoman starts reminiscing, once she has a captive audience, there is no stopping her. Take Mrs Dawson, Belfast born and bred, Allus to her friends. Let's give the lady her head and see what happens.

'Know what ah'm goin' till tell ye? Ah fairly miss ar wee shap. Many's the time ah think about it. It was a shap an' a half so it was. It wus at the corner. Wee Mrs McClinty run it. A grate wee woman. Her man died with his chest an' there she was — left. All on her loan she was, for there was no fambly.

'Bein' a widda woman she had to do somethin' so she started a wee shap in her own house. Everybody was that sarry for her they tried to give her a haun, like. She tuk aff first wi' the kendy apples. She wud put a dozen av them on a plate in the winda an' when they were sowl out the shap shut for she had nathin' else till sell. That wus at the start. In a wee while she started to spread her wings and ye cud buy kali suckers and black balls. Then she went intil the yella man and the next thing it wus potted herns, the *Weekly Welcome* and the *Christian Herald*.

'Anyway one thing led till another an' lo an' behold she moves till the shap at the corner when owl Harbison the grocer makes up his mine till errigate to Canada. Before ye knew she had made it intil a grate wee place. Sweetie mice an' liquorice laces, and corn squares. There wus tatie bread forby. It wud hev melted in yer mouth so it would. They come from all over the Chankil for it. She had a go at Madeera cake but giv' it up. She said there wus no future in that end of the business.

'Then she tuk up the grocery end in a big way. Things like ham enns and pig's feet, self-raisin' flour and tinned peas. Ach there wus no stappin' her.

If ye ast fer it an' she didden hev it she wud hev it the nex' time ye went in. She was awful obligin'. She wus the kine of woman that if ye ast for broken biscuits she wud think' nathin of breakin' some jes till oblige ye.

'Roun' about this time she tried to get the po staffis but somebody else gat it. She wus terrible put out but she sojered on and in the enn she did all right without it. She always kep stamps, tho. If ye wanted a stamp on a Sardy night she wud sell it till ye.

'She knew everybody that came in. She always had a good word for them, whether it wus a wee chile buying dolly mixtures or a woman luckin' corn beef. There wus Mrs Shoos. I mine the day she landed in at the time she wus expectin' her first. A woman in a the shap said till her, "Maggie, ye aren't goin' till have a baby are ye?" Like a flash Mrs McClinty comes out with, "What a question till ast. D'ye think she's carryin' that for a fren?"

'The rhubarb jam Mrs McClinty made herself wus outa this world, so it was. We all went mad about it in our house. M'da thought it was fantastic. An' ah mine her loose lentils. Ye nivver see loose lentils these days, d'ye? M'ma wud send me till the wee shap for the messages. I loved till go. Ach it wus like yesterday. Things like a ha'porth of aniseed balls for m'da's cough and a quarter av middlin' fat ham cut thin. She kep owl *Tellies* for wrappin' up the vegetables but she had nice clean begs for thing like rice and sugar. Ye always knew a beg that came from the wee shap for it wus covered wi' figures. Mrs McClinty wud use them for addin' up yer bill. She had a wee stub av a pencil an' she wus always lickin' it. When there wus a rush on she always said, "I'm goin' a right lick this mornin'."

'I mine owl Mrs Oswald who was nivver outa the place, chitterin' away there like she wus woun' up. She wus as mean as pirty oaten and wus always gettin' a quarter of bacon cut thin for her man's dinner. She always said it was for his bowels. I cud nivver understand how it cud help his bowels.

'Ach that wee shap, I can see ivvery bit of it in my mine's eye. I 'member the slimmin' biscuits that Mrs Cluney said were grate between a soda farl. I mine the laxatives too. Mrs McClinty wud always say, "Don't ever take a laxative for a cough. It nivver works." One day when she said it a customer towl her back, "Begod Mrs McClinty, it has this time. There's a wee man stannin' here beside me and he's frightened out of his wits till cough."

'If ivver anybody wanted credit Mrs McClinty wud laugh an' tell them, "Nivver bar yer head astin'. Sure the Wee Shap Association wud hev my life if they ivver heard I giv credit. Ah might as well shut the place down this minnit. Nobody wud give *me* credit. I cudn't giv' it till anybody else, God help me. I can just about scrape a livin' outa this place an' no more. It takes me all my time. See me? I hev as much chance of makin' a fortune outa this wee shap here as av being made the Lady Mayoress."

'She had a far out cousin who was forever at her to make more of the place, as he said. He was always tellin' her about what he called the patentshal. Yer nat makin' enough av it, he said. Every shap has an annual sale, he towl her. It's grate fer business. People think they're gettin' a bargain and this makes them buy more. It wus wee buns, he said. So one day he wrote a notice in big letters fer yer to put in the winda. It said:

ANNUAL SALE — EVERYTHING BROUGHT DOWN

When the customers ast her what kine of things wur any cheaper than any other day she just towl them EVERYTHING wus cheaper. They'd just have to take her word for it, "Ye know me," she said. They all said she wus the quare geg but she just laffed at them an' said she'd be mad if she thought she cud pull the wool over anybody's eyes. She just wusn't that kine av a wumman. There was a fella went in and ast her with a straight face if he cud hev a pair av trousers. She chased him so she did. Ach but it wus all the grate crack.

'Know what I'm goin' till tell ye? M'da thought there wus no place in the wide worl' like the wee shap. See him? Give him lashins av dip and he was as happy as Larry. He thought the worl' av Mrs McClinty's sodas. He was dyin' about ribs an' onions on a Sardy night and his broth of a Sunda'. Bacon knees an' ham shanks were all the same to him, just as long as there wus plenty av fat on them. The wee shap was quaren handy when he wud come home late from the coal quay and there wus nathin' for his supper.

'Ye wud nivver tire of hearin' about the things people went till the wee shap fer. Mrs Tully, ni. Her man had a wooden leg. She was always lamentin' about the spuds. They were that small they were like Beecham's Pills she said. Then there wus the wee lad from the bottom of the street who wud always ast for a pan and say, "But it's one till ate an' not till fry with."

'People used to complain that it was awful cowl if they had to stan' about waitin'. She wud just laff at them and say, "See me? Ah know its cowler than Greenland's icy mountains but sure its good for trade. It keeps people from just stannin' there gossipin' instead of buyin'." There wus a woman who raised Cain one day about the milk. It was aff, she said. "Missus," Mrs McGlinty towl her, "that milk was grass only a coupla hours ago. Its not a word of a lie."

"Mrs Chasty wus nivver outa the place. Mrs Chasty had five of a fambly, all boys. "They ate me outa house an' home," she wud say. "They go through them spuds like they were nivver goin' till see another bite. All I can do is just stan' there astin' myself where in the name av God they put them all. Ach all the same ye wudden be without them."

'Rite enough there was nobody like wee Mrs McGlinty. No matter what time of the night ye gat her up she wud come till the dure and get ye what ye wanted, whether it was salt or a stummick powder, a quarter av flour or a packet av starch. She used till sell corn plasters that worked like magic. "It isn't the way I wrap things up," she wud say. "It's obligin' the customers. That's what counts."

'Anyway we went till live at the other end of town and it was a quare while before I was back in the street again visitin' a fren. I sez till myself ah'll go down and take a luck at the wee shap again, to see if it wus still there for they said Mrs McGlinty was dead and buried. So ah walked down till the corner and there it was. Gone. Ach ah stud there an' nearly cried my eyes out. The whole street wus all knocked down. There was nathin' left. Nathin' but a lock of owl breeks. Nathin' but a bit av waste groun'.

'So ah said to myself, thinking of poor wee Mrs McGlinty, thinkin' of her dolly mixtures and her loose lentils, rememberin' her kendy apples and the corn plasters, "Ach but it's sad," I thought till myself. "If ye were only here ni. Isn't it funny? The notice yer cousin wrote for you that time. It's true at last. EVERYTHING BROUGHT DOWN."'

What's your rating in the Norn Iron chart?

It takes more than an accent to expose the genuine Ulsterman. Other characteristics betray him as effectively as his speech.

The true blue Ulsterman, for example, feels no remorse over his inborn attitudes, and tends to treat with a degree of contempt the codes of decorum rigidly observed elsewhere.

As this is the age of the self-analysis test it is interesting to draw on the help of the device in identifying the genuine article with reasonable accuracy.

To check whether you speak and act like an Ulsterman born and bred answer these questions with honesty:

1. If you want to cast doubt on someone's sanity which of these labels would you give him?
    (a) 'A quare geg'
    (b) 'A stupa ijit'

(c) 'An oddity'.

2. When speaking of the woman you married which of these expressions do you use?
   (a) 'The wife'
   (b) 'The missus'
   (c) 'My wife'.

3. When you want to pass someone in a crowded shop which of these do you say?
   (a) 'Excuse me.'
   (b) 'Would you let me by.'
   (c) Or do you say nothing and push past.

4. What is your reaction to an Irish joke? Does it
   (a) Irritate you.
   (b) Amuse you.
   (c) Affect you in the same way as any joke.

5. Which do you say when describing something you have just experienced?
   (a) 'It happened ther ni.'
   (b) 'It was a wee while ago.'
   (c) 'It's only after happening.'

6. How long since you have attended a wake?
   (a) A week or two ago.
   (b) Many years ago.
   (c) Never.

7. If rain is predicted which precaution do you take?
   (a) Carry an umbrella.
   (b) Carry a raincoat over your arm, or over your shoulder.
   (c) Carry both.

8. When you are explaining something which do you add at the end?
   (a) 'You understand.'
   (b) 'Y'know.'
   (c) 'Like y'know.'

9. You are seated in a crowded bus and a woman laden with parcels stands challengingly over you. How do you react?
   (a) Offer her your seat, saying nothing.
   (b) Rise, saying, 'Take the weight off your legs.'
   (c) Stay where you are.

10. You bring out a cigarette and discover you have no matches. What step do you take?
    (a) Gesture silently with it towards the first cigarette smoker you meet?
    (b) Stop him, saying 'Givvus a light?'
    (c) Wave your cigarette at him and ask 'I wonder if you'd mind?'

11. You encounter a woman motorist who has had a puncture. What would you do?
    (a) Stop and offer to help.
    (b) Go on your way, ignoring her.
    (c) Ask her if she would like you to ring the AA.

Now check your score with the following table of points
    1. a = 3, b = 2, c = 1.   2. a = 3, b = 2, c = 1.   3. a = 1, b = 3, c = 2.
    4. a = 1, b = 3, c = 2.   5. a = 3, b = 2, c = 1.   6. a = 3, b = 2, c = 1.
    7. a = 1, b = 2, c = 3.   8. a = 1, b = 2, c = 3.   9. a = 1, b = 3, c = 1.
    10. a = 3, b = 2, c = 1.   11. a = 1, b = 2, c = 3.

Your rating can now be worked out as follows: 16-33 — you are an average Ulsterman. 8-16 — you behave like an Ulsterman when you aren't thinking. 0-8 — You may be an Ulsterman born and bred but you try to forget it.

Here is a rating chart designed specially for the ladies:

1. You learn that an unexpected visitor is about to call. You don't know them too well and you are wearing curlers. How do you act?
    (a) Do you dash to take the curlers out?
    (b) Do you hastily cover them with a scarf?
    (c) Do you let them stay as they are?
2. If you are out for a walk with your husband and baby and you ask him to wheel the pram, what would you expect him to do?
    (a) Take it over from you quite naturally.
    (b) Agree but be aware he felt awkward about it.
    (c) Tell you he would rather not.
3. What do you reply when asked about the state of your health?
    (a) 'I'm feeling a bit off.'
    (b) 'Ah'm away till scrapins.'
    (c) 'Ah'm not at myself.'
4. What do you do when you meet a stranger on a country road?
    (a) Say 'Good morning.'
    (b) Give him a friendly nod.
    (c) Ignore him.
5. You have a little girl who insists on drawing attention to herself. Which do you do?
    (a) Order her to behave.
    (b) Tell her, 'You're making an exhibition of yourself.'
    (c) Complain, 'You're driving me astray in the head.'

6. Which would you say when commenting about a showery day?
   (a) 'Smizzlin.'
   (b) 'Spittin'.'
   (c) 'It's started to rain.'
7. If you wanted to praise someone which would you say?
   (a) 'He's stickin' out.'
   (b) 'He's fairly gettin' on.'
   (c) 'He's doing rather well.'

Use this table to check your score —
   1. a = 1, b = 2, c = 4.   2. a = 1, b = 2, c = 3.   3. a = 1, b = 2, c = 3.
   4. a = 1, b = 2, c = 3.   5. a = 1, b = 3, c = 2.   6. a = 3, b = 4, c = 1.
   7. a = 4, b = 2, c = 1.

Your rating can now be worked out as follows: 16-24 — you can look on yourself as a typical Ulsterwoman. 8-16 — You are an average Ulsterwoman but a shade conscious of it. 0-8 — You may be average at heart but you try to disguise it.

Glossary Mark III

This glossary covers many of the words used in the preceding pages. It is not intended to be all-embracing and is best used in conjunction with those which appeared in *What a Thing to Say* and *See Me See Her*.

It should be noted that Ulster speech includes many expressions confined to particular areas and almost unknown outside them. Many are used chiefly by the older generation.

ACK	Expresses impatience, eg 'Ack I know him but I can't think of his name.'
ACHAWAY OR THON	'I don't believe you.' *See also* AWAYORTHON.
AGAYON	Again, eg 'We're going back there agayon.'
AHAFTA	I have to, eg 'Ahafta go now.'
ANTIZE	Antagonise.
AMAWAYON	I have gone, eg 'Amayon back to the house.'
AMFERBEDNI	I am now going to bed.
ASTIN	Asking.
ATTERSELF	State of health, eg 'She's nat atterself.'
AWAYORTHON	Don't be absurd.
BLINEASABAT	Almost sightless, eg 'The referee's blineasabat.'
BOGGIN	Dirty, untidy, eg 'The room was boggin'.'
BOOKIE	Bunch of flowers; bouquet, eg 'He gave his wife a bookie for their anniversity.'
BULLY	Good, eg 'Bully Jimmy'; otherwise, 'It's good to see you.'
BULK	Flick with the fingers, eg 'He can fairly bulk marleys.'
BUNSE UP	Go Dutch; share the bill.
BURR	Butter.
CAST UP	Recall unkindly, eg 'She cast up that owl jumper she giv' me an' I just tuk it an' hit her up the bake wi' it.
CHILE	Child.
COLD FOOL	Cold chicken, eg 'I'm dyin' about cold fool on a warm day.'

CRIBBIN	Kerb, eg 'I cribbed my toe on the cribbin.'
DEED	Passed away, eg 'He's deed and gone.'
DICLAS	Ridiculous, eg 'That's a diclas thing to say.'
DOIN UP	Decorating, eg 'We're gettin' the house done up.'
EGGY	Agnes, eg 'Ar Eggy's a quare wee dancer.'
ENN	End, eg 'It was that cowl last night I nearly caught my enn.'
ESSET	Is it, eg 'How much esset?'
FAIRLY	Excellent, eg 'That wee lad can fairly run.'
FARR	Father.
FLAFF	Wave about, also fall off. eg 'He flaffa lather.'
FLIAN	Flying, eg 'He was flian because he won a prize at the pools.'
FOAM	Telephone, eg 'Our wee budgie loves to sit on the foam.'
FREN	Friend.
FURNIKURE	Furniture.
GEESALITE	Could you give me a match?
GUFF	Cheek, impertinence, eg 'Don't give me any of yer owl guff.'
HAEYEAW'WIYE	Have you everything with you?
HARP SIX	Tumble, eg 'He went harp six on the pavement.'
HAUN	Hand, eg 'You're takin' a haun outa me.'
HAVERS	Share, eg 'We'll go havers on the bill.'
HICE	House, eg 'We're livin' in an awful nice wee hice ni.'
HI EWE	Look here, I say there.
IRES	Hours, eg 'He sits on his behine for ires.'
JAPS	Mud spots, eg 'Them japs always ruin me tights.'
KIDLEYS	Kidneys.

KISSICK	Kiosk.
LACK	Like, eg 'Lack ye know.'
LAKE	Leak, eg 'There's a lake in the kettle.'
LETTININ	Leaking, eg 'My shoes are lettinin.'
LATHER	Ladder.
MAJAREEN	Margarine.
MENDED	Improved in health; repaired, eg 'You're lookin' awful well mended.'
MIZZLIN	Mizzling, raining gently, eg 'It's been mizzlin' for nearly half an hour.'
NEUCK	Steal, eg 'The wee lad neucked an orange at the fruit shop.'
NOTIONATE	To blow hot and cold.
OMANEXORE	My neck is hurting.
OMANEES	I have hurt my knees.
ONEDAY	Window, eg 'They broke our oneday.'
OWLIG	Old fool.
OWLIP	Abuse, eg 'Don't give me any of yer owlip.'
PLANE	Playing.
PIJUNS	Pigeons, eg 'Them pijuns breed like black taxis.'
PRAVINZ	Province; Northern Ireland.
RITE SHAR	Fairly heavy shower of rain.
RIZ	Got up.
SALLRITE	Satisfactory.
SCRETCH	Scratch, eg 'I got a scretch on my henn.'
SCUNNER	Dislike, eg 'I took a scunner at her.'
SKELP	Slap, eg 'That wee girl needs a good skelp.'
SLABBER	Untrustworthy person, eg 'He's a right slabber.'
SPITTER	Bitterly cold.
STEEMIN	Teeming; training, eg 'Steemin' again, so it is.'
STICKINOUT	Excellent, eg 'He's stickinout.'

STURE	Dust.
SWALLY	Swallow.
SENFIR	Sent for, eg 'When I saw the car coming straight at me I thought I was senfir.'
TATIE	Potato, eg 'I'm dyin' about tatie bread.'
THEMINS	Those persons, eg 'Themins is at it again.'
THERNI	Just recently, a little while ago, eg 'It happened thereni.'
THEREYARNI	There you are now, otherwise 'Let that be a lesson to you.'
THEWAFF	Vomited, took sick.
TILET	Toilet, eg 'I'm lookin' for the tilet. Where is it?'
TITTALY	Italy, eg 'She went Tittaly for her holidays.'
TRACE	Terrace, eg 'He lives in a trace house.'
VAMITIN	Sick, see 'Thewaff'.
VILEIN	Violin, eg 'The wee lad's a quare haun on the vilein.'
WALLACE	Waltz, eg 'May I have this wallace?'
WEGOTANORN	We got another one.
WHEEKER	Superior, eg 'My new car's a wheeker.'
WINDY STOOL	Window sill.
WIR	Our, eg 'We are going home to have wir tea.'
WIRE	Weather, eg 'This wire's desperate.'
WUNCENFERALL	My final word, eg 'I'm tellin' you wuncenferall. I'm finished.'
WUNNEN	Stand up, eg 'Get on your wunnen and we'll go home.'
YERINFERITNI	You have it coming to you.